Mutts

ABDO
Publishing Company
A Buddy Book
by
Julie Murray

VISIT US AT
www.abdopublishing.com

Published by Buddy Books, an imprint of ABDO Publishing Company, 8000 West 78th Street, Edina, Minnesota 55439. Copyright © 2003 by Abdo Consulting Group, Inc. International copyrights reserved in all countries. No part of this book may be reproduced in any form without written permission from the publisher.

Printed in the United States of America, North Mankato, Minnesota.
012003 102010
Edited by: Christy DeVillier
Contributing Editors: Matt Ray, Michael P. Goecke
Graphic Design: Maria Hosley
Image Research: Deborah Coldiron
Cover Photograph: Eyewire, Inc.
Interior Photographs: Eyewire, Inc., Photodisc, Photospin

Library of Congress Cataloging-in-Publication Data

Murray, Julie, 1969-
  Mutts/Julie Murray.
      p. cm. — (Animal kingdom)
  Summary: Simply describes the characteristics of dogs that are of mixed breed and how to care for them.
  ISBN 1-57765-641-5
      1. Mutts (Dogs)—Juvenile literature. [1. Dogs. 2. Pets.] I. Title. II. Animal kingdom (Edina, Minn.)

SF426.5 .M85 2002
636.7'0887—dc21

                                      2001041252

Contents

Dogs

People have kept dogs as pets for over 10,000 years. Dogs are relatives of the wild wolf. Nobody is sure how dogs became tame.

Today, there are over 100 different dog **breeds**. A few dog breeds are greyhounds, Great Danes, and beagles.

Dogs have been our friends
for thousands of years.

What Is A Mutt?

A **purebred** dog belongs to one **breed**. Two different purebreds will have a **crossbreed** puppy. A purebred and a crossbreed will have a **mongrel**. Two mongrels will have a mutt. Two crossbreeds will have mutts, too. And, of course, two mutts will have mutt puppies.

What Makes A Mutt?

Mongrel

Mongrel

Crossbreed

Crossbreed

Mutt

Mutt

Mutt

What They Are Like

Mutts are common pets. They can be smarter, stronger, and healthier than **purebred** dogs. Some people believe mutts are friendlier, too. Every dog, purebred or mutt, is special in its own way.

All-American is another name for the mutt.

What Mutts Look Like

Mutts come in all sizes. They can be small like poodles and weigh only 10 pounds (5 kg). Mutts can be big like German shepherds and weigh 100 pounds (45 kg). Mutts can be medium-sized dogs, too.

A mutt's hair can be long or short and any color.

A mutt's coat can be any color. Their hair may be long or short. Mutts can have coats of straight hair or wavy hair. A mutt's hair may be soft and furry or rough and scratchy.

Grooming And Care

A dog should be brushed at least once a week. Brushing keeps a mutt's coat smooth and clean. Most dogs only need a few baths each year. Someone should clip a dog's nails as needed. Cleaning your dog's teeth is a good idea, too.

Dogs need baths.

Like people, dogs need a doctor's care to stay healthy. It is important to take your mutt to a **veterinarian**.

Feeding And Exercise

All dogs need food and fresh water every day. Follow the feeding directions on your dog's food bag. Try not to change your dog's type of food too often. A changing **diet** can lead to health problems.

Give your mutt food and
fresh water every day.

All dogs need exercise. Some mutts need more exercise than others do. Playing "fetch" outside may be enough for some dogs. Other dogs may need a long walk every day. Older dogs may need less exercise.

Some mutts love to play "fetch".

Puppies

Between three and six puppies are commonly born in a mutt's litter. Newborn puppies are blind and deaf. They will begin seeing and hearing at about two weeks old. Puppies should not leave their mothers before they are seven or eight weeks old.

Mutt puppies can grow up to be small dogs or big dogs.

It is hard to tell what a mutt puppy will look like when it is full grown. It could look like its mother or father. Or a mutt may not look like its parents at all.

Puppy School

Puppy schools can help you train your puppy. You can teach your puppy commands like "sit" and "stay." At puppy school, your dog can meet other dogs and people. This is an important part of training a puppy.

Important Words

breed a special group of dogs. Dogs of the same breed look alike.

crossbreed a puppy of two different purebred dogs.

diet the food that a dog (or a person) normally eats.

litter a group of puppies born at one time.

mongrel a puppy of a purebred and a crossbreed.

purebred describes a dog that belongs to only one breed.

veterinarian a doctor for animals. A short name for veterinarian is "vet."

Web Sites

k9web!

www.k9web.com
Find people to help you care for your dog by
visiting this site.

The Joy of Mutts

www.geocities.com/heartland/hills/5441
This site is dedicated to the mutt. See the "Mutt
of the Month" or guess which breeds make up a
mutt from the photo album.

Dog-Play

www.dog-play.com
Learn about different activities for you and your
dog. From games to training exercises, this site
shows you how to get started.

Index